D0590777

YOU KNOW YOU'RE A FOOTBALL FANATIC WHEN...

Summersdale Publishers Ltd
46 West Street
Chichester
West Sussex
PO19 1RP
UK

www.summersdale.com

Printed and bound in China

ISBN: 978 1 84953 046 0

Substantial discounts on bulk quantities of Summersdale books are available to corporations, professional associations and other organisations. For details telephone Summersdale Publishers on (+44-1243-771107), fax: (+44-1243-786300) or email (nicky@summersdale.com).

You Know You're a
Football Fanatic
When...

Ben Fraser

summersdale

You Know You're a
Football Fanatic
When...

You paint your satellite dish the same colour as your football strip... to blend in with the colour of your house.

Your very first words were, 'Who are ya? Who are ya?'

Billy Elliot had you in tears for weeks...
how could a boy like ballet but
not football?

If you can't get to sleep, you count goals, not sheep.

You plan on calling your kids David Beckham, Christiano Ronaldo and Fernando Torres. Even if they're girls.

You eat Walkers Crisps just to be that extra bit closer to Gary Lineker.

When asked to wear your Sunday best,
you turn up in your team's
football strip.

You have lines painted on your lawn so it resembles a pitch, and shout at the dog when he goes offside.

You cancel your wedding because it clashes with an important match, then decide to be romantic after all and squeeze it in during half-time.

You dump your girlfriend because she thinks Aston Villa is a posh holiday house.

You think rugby is a dirty word.

When most toddlers had a comfort blanket, you had a saliva-stained football scarf. It's really time to replace it.

You refuse to go into higher education because The Open University doesn't do a degree in Footballology.

You stopped buying the *Sunday Sport*...
because there wasn't enough
sport in it.

Your bed linen is covered with skid marks... because you wear your football boots in bed.

If you die (probably in a tragic footballing accident), it won't be your life that flashes before your eyes but the 100 greatest goals of all time.

You regard yourself as having a wide circle of friends whom you spend quality time with each week... but whether or not the other 10,000 supporters in the stadium are even aware of your existence is another matter.

You apply the rules of football to your life very successfully... You're currently sitting on the sidelines.

One of your top chat-up lines is: 'Hey, I've got a really heavy tackle – do you want to see?' You then proceed to kick the person in the knees.

You get a job painting the roads just so you can tell your friends that you're a linesman.

Your lover leaves you because you and your mates have made one too many smutty innuendoes about her penalty box.

Your best chat-up line includes an explanation of the offside rule. And still you wonder why it hasn't worked.

You tried to time the births of all your children with the birthdays of famous footballers. It's surprising you even had the chance to conceive, given your chat-up lines.

Your top sexual fantasy would be...
fantasy football.

Your maths teacher at school suggested you stick to division... as in First, Second and Third.

Your entire CD collection consists of World Cup and football songs. You consider 'Nice One Cyril' to be the best record of all time.

You think football WAGs are the greatest invention since... football.

You sing football chants to your baby
instead of lullabies.

You take up gardening so that
your herbaceous borders match
your team colours. However, when
there's a drought, you have to switch
allegiances from Yeovil Town to
Norwich City.

You are trying to get Emirates,
Samsung and AIG to sponsor your kids.

You'd rather score a goal than score
in bed.

You accept a job when the employer tells you they'll pay for your season ticket... but when they offer you a year's worth of travel cards instead you take them to an industrial tribunal.

You just can't understand why people take the mick out of the monarchy. What have Posh and Becks done to deserve that?

You proudly boast that you're on your local team's reserve list... of people they might allow to join their fan club.

You kill a pig and inflate its bladder... just so you can see how it was for medieval players of the game.

You'd like to be buried under your team's pitch.

You've been sacked from all previous employment for knowing 'sweet FA'. What's wrong with having nothing but an extensive knowledge of the Football Association?

Your girlfriend threatens to leave because you care more about Chelsea than you do about her. Without intending to be mean, you point out that you care more about Accrington Stanley than you do about her.

Your idea of foreplay is a quick dribble.

You cry in your stadium seat before the World Cup match even starts... because you've left your flag-coloured face paints at home.

If you were making a period drama, you'd cast Vinnie Jones as the hero and David Ginola as the heroine.

You commission a life-size portrait of
your favourite footballer.

Your greatest personal success is nearly beating Brazil... on your PlayStation. You came a valiant second.

You want plastic surgery. After all, two right feet would definitely make you twice the striker you already are.

Your favourite film would have to be
20,000 Premier Leagues Under The Sea.

Your idea of a good poem is... anything
by Eric Cantona.

You had a mental breakdown
when your prescription – whoops:
subscription – to Sky Sports was
inadvertently cancelled.

At your wedding, the bride walks down the aisle to the tune of 'Three Lions' and the reception is held at a local sports shop.

You decorate the walls at home with
banners, not pictures.

You would have liked George Best to be godfather to one of your kids. What a fine example he would have made.

You hide your Arsenal Ladies programmes beneath your stash of dirty magazines.

You learned to read at quite a young age, but only because your dad was into *Roy of the Rovers*.

You don't think football trivia is trivial. I mean, surely everyone needs to know that Alvin Martin also ran an office furniture business?

Your little boy asks for some transfers for his birthday and you send him and his sister to a foster home.

Your girlfriend repeatedly tries to dump you and you don't get the message until she flashes you a red card.

You have a broad vocabulary of swear words but try to book anyone who uses foul language against you.

You receive a ten-match touchline ban for screaming abuse at your kids who are playing in an Under-7s game.

You learned the alphabet very quickly.
After all, UEFA only has four letters.

You invest your life savings in shares in your football club to help them afford the new star striker they desperately need.

Your mobile ringtone sounds
suspiciously like the theme tune for
Match of the Day.

Your neck is stained in the colours of your team scarf.

You nip into a church when you hear chanting as you pass, thinking it's an indoor footie match, but leave when you notice that for some reason the referee is wearing a cassock.

You give the referee the address of the nearest optician at the end of a match.

Your team is 5–1 up in the last ten minutes but you still can't relax until the final whistle.

Your idea of a gourmet lunch at the game is a pie with actual meat in it.

You think jumpers were invented for
the sole purpose of being used
as goalposts.

You have replaced family photos with those of your favourite team.

All your holidays are planned around European tournaments... unless your team doesn't qualify, in which case there's no point in you having a holiday at all.

You have your house carpeted in
AstroTurf.

You trip over in the street and try to blame it on the person nearest to you. When they refuse to take responsibility you head butt them.

Your family move abroad while you're watching the cup final and you don't even notice.

You're happy to be seen out and about
in a ridiculous bobble hat in your
team's colours – even in the
heat of summer.

Have you enjoyed this book?
If so, why not write a review
on your favourite website?

Thanks very much for buying
this Summersdale book.

www.summersdale.com